35 QUESTIONS FOR THOSE WHO HATE THE PROSPERITY GOSPEL

ALSO FROM REVIVAL TODAY

Financial Overflow

Dominion Over Sickness and Disease

Boldly I Come

Twenty Secrets for an Unbreakable Marriage

How to Dominate in a Wicked Nation

Seven Wrong Relationships

Everything a Man Should Be

Understanding the World in Light of Bible Prophecy

Are You Going Through a Crisis?

The 20 Laws that Govern the Financial Anointing

35 Questions for Those Who Hate the Prosperity Gospel

Books are available in EBOOK and PAPERBACK through your favorite online book retailer or by request from your local bookstore.

35 QUESTIONS FOR THOSE WHO HATE THE PROSPERITY GOSPEL

JONATHAN SHUTTLESWORTH

Book design by eBook Prep
www.ebookprep.com

December 2023
ISBN: 978-1-64457-661-8

Rise UP Publications
644 Shrewsbury Commons Ave
Ste 249
Shrewsbury PA 17361
United States of America
www.riseUPpublications.com
Phone: 866-846-5123

CONTENTS

"Don't let religion neuter you. Dream big, do big. You can believe for God's best...you can have God's best."

— JONATHAN SHUTTLESWORTH

INTRODUCTION

You'll have a hard time naming four people who had more first-time decisions for Christ in their ministry than T.L. Osborn. He wrote the following in his book, *The Power of Positive Desire: Seven Vital Principles For Unlimited Living*:

> *IF EVERYONE would use God's laws, discipline themselves, and go for life's best, the "privileged" few would cease to monopolize the good life. The so-called "underprivileged" majority would transform themselves by God's principles and the successful life would be shared by the many.*
>
> *Religions say, "Beware! Material affluence—or even sufficiency may corrupt or spoil people."*
>
> *This demeaning assault on Christian minds began during the Dark Ages.*
>
> *An unprejudiced study of early Christianity reveals the practice of positive faith for God's abundant lifestyle. They prospered and they were generous.*
>
> *Then Constantine's acceptance of Christ popularized Christianity. Following this epoch, a dominating church hierarchy evolved to*

*control business, science, education, and religion. Astute church
leaders manipulated public wealth until the religious system monop-
olized financial control, and the people were reduced to poverty
through tolls and taxes.*

*The masses became restless in their subservient role and asserted
their claim to a better life. That was when financial experts of the
church hierarchy consorted with the clergy to invent doctrines which
would sanctify poverty and thus pacify the peasantry.*

*Invoking God, they brainwashed the people who were not allowed to
read the Bible. Their mischievous dictums advocated:*

That material poverty fosters spiritual humility;

*That prosperity or the good life motivates arrogance, pride, and
sinful living;*

*That ordinary people are not qualified to manage material wealth
without being infected by its potential malignancy.*

*To this day, many church dogmas, handed down from the medieval
period, are still proliferated, sanctifying poverty and stigmatizing
prosperity.*

*Bible teachings intended to discourage the perverted love of money,
have been twisted into threatening doctrines that material gain
produces arrogance and invites damnation.*

This is from Chapter 31 of the book *The Power of Positive Desire* by T.
L. Osborn. It's called the 'Oath of Prosperity':

*TRUE FAITH can only be based on God's plan, His ideas, His
dream. These are recorded in His word.*

*All that He wants from you is your daily reassurance that you
believe Him enough to stick to His desires regardless of the
influences or circumstances stacked against you.*

*If your faith is suppressed by negative teaching that to desire better
things and a better life is wrong, then you will waste your life and
die in resignation and pious failure.*

You will be like so many who have bound themselves with an oath of poverty. God never planned for anyone to do that. He planned prosperity.

It would be good if you would decide today to take an OATH OF PROSPERITY and say:

"I VOW never to be poor and in need again,
since my Father created the wealth of this
planet for me to enjoy.

"I VOW never to be unable to reach out
and lift others in need. God is in me
and He is rich.

"I VOW to always appropriate God's BEST
in life so that I can enjoy His abundance
myself and so I can share His abundance
with others in need."

The Lord is my shepherd; I refuse to lack. My cup of blessing runs over. (Psalm 23:1,5)

This is the lifestyle that God has planned for you.

———

Many are quick to say, "I hate the prosperity gospel. I hate the message of prosperity." Well, you've likely never been poor. I'm speaking as someone who has experienced poverty, confirmed by the state of Virginia when they mailed our state income taxes back to us with a letter basically saying, "In good conscience, we can't receive your and Adalis's tax money. We're returning your money. Please avail yourself of our state programs to help you get back on your feet."

Poverty is terrible. God didn't create people to be poor, and God didn't create people to be sick. Yet, as T.L. Osborn asserted, when Christianity got hijacked by the government, and Bible reading was forbidden for common people, church leaders and the government decided it would be best if people stayed poor because then they could take all their money for themselves. That's what happened.

But somehow, even after the Bible was released to the masses, there are still critics who, despite 2,000 Scriptures on wealth, abundance, and stewardship, still have harsh things to say about prosperity. The harsh things they have to say are seldom challenged, but that changes with this book.

People hate the prosperity message, although most won't actually say so. This is the case in America, the Western world—in Europe, and throughout Canada. There are many preachers who, if someone asked them, "Are you a prosperity preacher?" They would say, "No, I'm not a prosperity preacher." They would immediately distance themselves in response. And these same preachers wonder why they don't have any money. You'll never have the things you speak against.

There are harsh critics of prosperity within the Church, and I have 35 questions for these critics, many of which they can't answer. I have a unique background than most preachers. I was not raised in "faith churches." I was raised in "anti-faith" churches, or at best, churches where they mix together a little faith with some unbelief.

I went to a Bible college that was steeped in unbelief. They warned me about prosperity preachers and the so-called "prosperity gospel." I know how they think because I used to think that way, too. Unfortunately, for the Devil who wanted to keep me poor, I read the Bible and was privileged to be around men who didn't believe like me. And when I heard the Word of God from them concerning prosperity, it made total sense.

People who criticize the prosperity message are some of the stupidest people that you'll ever meet because nothing they say makes sense—I'm going to show you that. I have 35 questions for those who hate the prosperity message. These critics have never sat and thought about what they believe. Instead, they spend time around other like-minded people who just repeat the same things.

They usually start with this one: "It's easier for a camel to go through the eye of a needle than it is for a rich man to get into Heaven."

Just like T.L. Osborn said, they twist a few Scriptures to make the Bible say what it doesn't say.

The reason I have such harsh things to say is because the attack against prosperity is not academic; the attack is demonic. The Bible says in Psalm 112, *Silver and gold will be in the house of the righteous.* At the end of the Psalm, it says, *The wicked will see it and will gnash their teeth with rage.*

Many readers of this book are people who have completed Bible school, gone into full-time ministry, and put their hand to the plow but turned back due to lack of money. They worked with pastors who thought it was good to pay them nothing. They struggled for a while and couldn't make it. They couldn't provide for their wife or couldn't provide for their children. Other preachers have had that same attack but have overcome it. It's a work of the Devil to choke out the finances of the Church.

Anyone with an honest heart and a functioning brain can readily see that the world celebrates prosperity everywhere except prosperity in the church. The people who hate the prosperity of the Church really hate the Church itself and wish the Church didn't exist. They know the Church holds back the global anti-Christ system, which is prophesied in Revelation. They know the Church can't function without money.

Nobody has a problem with there being five intercontinental Islamic airlines. But if a Christian gets one jet, they become front-page news.

The dichotomy is demonic. If a sports betting parlor opens up in a city, the press reports it as if sports gambling was the greatest thing in the world. Meanwhile, kids' futures are gambled away by their fathers at a casino. There are fathers gambling away their child support payments, and their kids have to struggle. But the news showcases casinos in a good light. You'll never hear an exposé criticizing a casino owner for having a jet. Why does a man who manufactures beer and is indirectly responsible for the deaths of thousands of people every year live in a mansion? No one is upset about that. Why does he have a private aircraft? Yet, any minister of the gospel who gains any form of wealth is treated like the reincarnation of Hitler.

Unfortunately, I was born with a rare disease called "I don't give a crap what the world thinks about the Church." Let me put it this way: I don't care what the enemies of the Church think about the Church. And I don't care what the enemies of the gospel think is an acceptable level of prosperity for those who are born again.

My only concern is what God says in His Word. If God said I can have something He paid for, then I want it. If Jesus shed blood to enact a covenant, I want everything included in that covenant.

I already said that those who hate the prosperity message are among the stupidest people you'll ever meet; here's an example.

I have a friend whose wife was a stripper. After attending some of my meetings, they got married and fully committed their lives to the Lord. I thought they'd given their lives to the Lord beforehand, but they got really serious with God when I was in town after hearing me preach at the meetings.

Let me tell you how she ended up coming to church as a stripper. She was so repulsed by the wickedness of the American public school system and what was taught that she used the money she earned from stripping to put her kid in a Christian school. She wanted them to have a godly education because of how foul the public school system is.

Money is an enabler. Money enables you to provide for your family. God warned against people who wouldn't provide for their families. He said, *"They've left the faith and are worse than infidels."*

Do you think people should have to put their children in American public schools just to be taught there's no such thing as gender? That a family is whatever you want it to be? That marriage can be between a man and a man, a woman and a woman, a woman and two cats, or three men and a woman? Do you think that's what God wants? Or do you think people should be able to put their children in Christian schools if they desire and receive an excellent education?

It takes money to do that. Why doesn't everybody do the same as the woman I mentioned before? If private school was free, no one would attend public schools. It takes money, and people don't have that money. A lot of students go to Christian schools because of scholarships. How are the scholarships provided? By Christians who have an abundance of finances. Money makes it possible for a mom who doesn't want her kid indoctrinated with teaching from demons to go to a Christian school.

How brain-dead must someone become to not see the advantage of a righteous man having an abundance of resources? The more money a wicked person has, the worse off the world is. The more money a truly righteous person has, the better off the world is. For those who are quick to warn against the prosperity gospel and say, "I hate the prosperity message, I hate blessing," I have 35 questions that I'd like for them to answer, but they can't answer them.

This will also help those of you who grew up as I did in churches that spoke harshly against financial blessing. I hope you're not stupid enough to continue going to a church that bad-mouths blessing. You can't prosper while submitting yourself to teaching that goes against what you're contending for.

If you grew up in a family that was "anti-blessing," and you later went over to the winning side, and now your family treats you like you've left the faith and joined some kind of cult—this book will help you.

 I am a joint heir of Christ and all that He owns.

QUESTION 1

DID GOD SPEAK ABOUT PROSPERITY?

D id God speak about prosperity? Yes, He did, and He spoke favorably about it.

> *"If you fully obey the Lord your God and carefully keep all his*
> *commands that I am giving you today, the Lord your God will*
> *set you high above all the nations of the world. You will experi-*
> *ence all these blessings if you obey the Lord your God:*
> *Your towns and your fields*
> *will be blessed.*
> *Your children and your crops*
> *will be blessed.*
> *The offspring of your herds and flocks*
> *will be blessed.*
> *Your fruit baskets and breadboards*
> *will be blessed.*
> *Wherever you go and whatever you do,*
> *you will be blessed.*
> *"The Lord will conquer your enemies when they attack you. They*

will attack you from one direction, but they will scatter from you in seven!

"The Lord will guarantee a blessing on everything you do and will fill your storehouses with grain. The Lord your God will bless you in the land he is giving you.

"If you obey the commands of the Lord your God and walk in his ways, the Lord will establish you as his holy people as he swore he would do. Then all the nations of the world will see that you are a people claimed by the Lord, and they will stand in awe of you.

"The Lord will give you prosperity in the land he swore to your ancestors to give you, blessing you with many children, numerous livestock, and abundant crops. The Lord will send rain at the proper time from his rich treasury in the heavens and will bless all the work you do. You will lend to many nations, but you will never need to borrow from them. If you listen to these commands of the Lord your God that I am giving you today, and if you carefully obey them, the Lord will make you the head and not the tail, and you will always be on top and never at the bottom. You must not turn away from any of the commands I am giving you today, nor follow after other gods and worship them."

— DEUTERONOMY 28:1-14

God spoke clearly about prosperity, and as we see from the above passage, He said a lot about it. In this passage, He talks about prosperity on many levels. God promises to set His people *high above the nations of the world.* This is a larger level of blessing that has been poured out on the nation of America. Think about the prosperity that the United States has in relation to other countries. *Towns and fields* are an extension of the blessing to the community. Then there are endeavors of His people that are blessed, including the work they set their hands to, and *their travels wherever they go* are blessed. It goes on to talk about protection from enemies and the blessing in the homes of the believers, their livestock, and their children.

 ## God gave prosperity for obedience.

Also, an abundance of food is listed here. *Storehouses filled with grain* and *fruit baskets and breadboards* are mentioned. That's not just about needs being met. That is above and beyond basic needs. Referring to the storehouse—this is a surplus that requires a structure to be built to house the extra grain. Imagine—there are anti-prosperity people who have a full fridge and pantry stocked with bread, fresh fruit, and produce with plenty of snacks to spare! If that's not hypocritical, I don't know what is. There are countries where people are starving or where people eat one meal a day. In comparison, many Americans have three meals a day plus snacks. That's an abundance of food! I'm all for the blessing of God as laid out here in Deuteronomy 28, but for people who claim to be against it, some of them are ignorantly living it. Verse 10 touches on how the blessing is something that *all the nations of the world will see*, which means it's a visible blessing. Verse 11 plainly says *The Lord will give you prosperity.* Some might argue that prosperity means more than just money, but here it doesn't. The King James Bible says *The Lord will make thee plenteous in goods.* That's material wealth—a multiplication of material wealth! The New Living Translation uses the word "prosperity." Verse 12 says, *You will lend to many nations but you will never borrow.* What can we conclude from this? Did God speak favorably of prosperity? The answer is yes. Prosperity is not a term created in Tulsa, Oklahoma, in the 1960s. It's not an American gospel—Abraham wasn't even from Texas, and he was obviously prosperous!

QUESTION 2

DOES EL SHADDAI MEAN THE GOD OF "POVERTY" OR "JUST ENOUGH?"

I've heard Christians speak their mind on the topic of God meeting peoples' needs. One man shared, "I'm not saying that God wants people poor. I believe God will meet your basic needs." Is El Shaddai the God that meets basic needs? That's my question. You'll never follow a wrong doctrine if you stick to preaching and believing what God revealed about Himself through His names. How can you be anti-healing when He said in Exodus 15:26, *"I am the Lord, who heals you."* In the Hebrew text, the title "The Lord Who Heals You" is *Jehovah-Rapha.* Healing is not just what God does. It's who He is because it's part of His name. The same goes for the name El Shaddai.

And then He said in Genesis 17:1, *When Abram was ninety-nine years old, the Lord appeared to him and said, "I am El-Shaddai—'God Almighty.'"*

El Shaddai—Almighty God—it's found 218 times. "El" signifies "strong one," and "Shaddai" means "breasted one." This pictures God as the strong nourisher, strength giver, satisfier, and all-bountiful supplier of His people. Its first occurrence here reveals God as the fruitful one who was to multiply Abraham abundantly. The life-giver who restored life to Abraham and Sarah—who were both as good as dead as far as offspring was concerned. Through Him, they would have future offspring as the dust and the stars and the sand in number.

The God of more than enough.

El Shaddai also means the "many-breasted one." He's the God of more than enough. Does El Shaddai mean that God is the God of lack or of just enough? Or does it mean the "many-breasted one," the God that has too much provision for His children? It's not just a name. It's what He did and who He is.

> Now the Lord had said unto Abram, Get thee out of thy country,
>   and from thy kindred, and from thy father's house, unto a land
>   that I will show thee:
> And I will make of thee a great nation, and I will bless thee, and
>   make thy name great; and thou shalt be a blessing:
> And I will bless them that bless thee, and curse him that curseth
>   thee: and in thee shall all families of the earth be blessed.
> So Abram departed, as the Lord had spoken unto him;

— GENESIS 12:1-4 (KJV)

> And Abram was very rich in cattle, in silver, and in gold.

— GENESIS 13:2 (KJV)

Does El Shaddai mean the God of poverty or the God who supplies your basic needs? No, He's the many-breasted one, the God of more than enough, the God that makes you extremely fruitful and rich.

When someone takes issue with this, they usually begin with, "I believe…" or "I feel…" It's not important what you believe or what you feel. It's important what the Bible says. If the Bible is the highest authority on truth, and you claim to be a Christian, base your faith on the Bible. I've heard people argue, "Well, I just have seen so many people abuse the prosperity message." My response is, "Who cares?" That false portrayal doesn't change the truth.

Maybe the Devil amplifies the people who abuse the prosperity message so people back off of it entirely. Did you ever think of that? It's not important to me what other people do; it's important to me what the Bible says.

QUESTION 3

HOW DID GOD CREATE MAN IN THE BEGINNING, AND HOW WILL THINGS END?

W hen God created man, where did He put him? In the projects? In a trailer park, scrounging to survive? Or did He put him in a garden of abundance? The following passage in Genesis illustrates the time and care that God put into creating the Garden of Eden. The garden was a type of paradise. It says here that there were trees of every kind.

> And God said, "Let the earth sprout vegetation, plants yielding seed,
>   and fruit trees bearing fruit in which is their seed, each
>   according to its kind, on the earth." And it was so. The earth
>   brought forth vegetation, plants yielding seed according to their
>   own kinds, and trees bearing fruit in which is their seed, each
>   according to its kind. And God saw that it was good.
>
> — GENESIS 1:11, 12 (ESV)

Everything in the garden was free and available (except for what God commanded them not to eat). Imagine going to a grocery store and gathering thousands of dollars worth of certified organic, non-

GMO produce and then trying to leave without paying. Impossible! If you tried, you'd probably be arrested or taken to a mental institution. My point is the Lord provided the highest quality food to Adam and Eve, and it cost them nothing. Each plant was also created with seeds so that there would be a perpetual harvest. The food supply would never run out. He blessed and prospered them. If you had to put a price on the trees, produce, and upkeep, it'd easily be worth thousands of dollars.

Secondly, every type of plant was made available.

> *And God said, "Behold, I have given you every plant yielding seed that is on the face of all the earth, and every tree with seed in its fruit. You shall have them for food. And to every beast of the earth and to every bird of the heavens and to everything that creeps on the earth, everything that has the breath of life, I have given every green plant for food." And it was so.*
>
> — GENESIS 1:29, 30 (ESV)

In the United States, it's common for tropical fruits to be imported. For example, mangoes are imported from Mexico. There are exotic fruits and vegetables that only grow in certain regions of the globe—some of these are not easily obtained. The point is God made every seed available on the face of the earth available in one place, the Garden of Eden. Adam and Eve were surrounded by abundance. They received wealth in land, natural resources, and gold.

> *A river flowed out of Eden to water the garden, and there it divided and became four rivers. The name of the first is the Pishon. It is the one that flowed around the whole land of Havilah, where there is gold.*
>
> — GENESIS 2:10, 11(ESV)

We can clearly see the prosperity God provided for Adam and Eve and the state of the garden before the fall.

The intention the Lord had for their home on Earth was to mimic what was already in Heaven. You may be familiar with the Lord's prayer, but not everyone takes into account God's will for prosperity, which is built into it. Jesus set the example for what prayer should look like.

 Your Kingdom come, your will be done on earth as it is in Heaven.

Do people not realize that Jesus is literally teaching us to pray for things to be on earth the way they are in Heaven?

How will it be at the end? What does Heaven look like? Does it look like Detroit? Does it look like Mogadishu? Or does it have streets of gold? Are the gemstones a man uses to show his love to a woman used as fencing?

If God hates wealth, He must be miserable in Heaven. If you think God hates wealth and material opulence, have you considered what Heaven looks like? If you hate wealth, you will be miserable in Heaven...if you make it.

QUESTION 4

WAS JESUS POOR?

I hear people tritely criticize preachers, saying, "These guys fly around in jets. Jesus was poor."

Was He? I have some follow-up questions below in answer to that question.

WHAT DID THE WISE MEN BRING TO CHRIST'S BABY SHOWER?

Gold, frankincense, and myrrh. From His inception on Earth—though He was born in a manger—abundance began to manifest.

DID JESUS HAVE WEALTHY SUPPORTERS?

Soon afterward Jesus began a tour of the nearby towns and villages, preaching and announcing the Good News about the Kingdom of God. He took his twelve disciples with him, along with some women who had been cured of evil spirits and diseases. Among them were Mary Magdalene, from whom he had cast out seven demons; Joanna, the wife of Chuza, Herod's business manager; Susanna; and many others who were contributing from their own resources to support Jesus and his disciples.

— LUKE 8:1-3

Jesus was well provided for in His ministry.

DID JESUS HAVE A TREASURER?

What poor person has a treasurer? If you go to a trailer park to sell Girl Scout cookies and knock on the door in the poorest area of a rural town and ask, "Would you like to buy some cookies?" Do they say, "Let me talk to my treasurer"? No, because they don't have a treasure that requires a treasurer.

 Jesus operated at a high level.

The fact that one disciple had to watch over the money and carry the money bag tells you that Jesus had an abundance of finances, let alone the fact that the Bible says that the disciple often stole from it for his own use (John 12:6). Yet, it never affected their ability to travel and minister. You know you have a lot of money when your treasurer is stealing from you, and it never affects one thing the ministry is doing.

DID JESUS TRAVEL WITH 12 MEN?

You can't travel alone when you're broke, let alone take 12 people with you—not counting the women who also traveled with Him.

DID JESUS SLEEP OUT IN THE DIRT?

He said He had no pillow to lay His head on. Jesus was speaking figuratively. The Bible says when they crossed over on the boat, Jesus was asleep with His head on a pillow. Do you think Jesus slept for three and a half years with His head on the ground? And then, when they said, *"Master, where are you staying?"* He didn't say, *"Well, I don't have any place to stay."* He said, *"Come and see,"* and the crowd pressed into the house.

WAS JESUS POOR?

You don't see Jesus living in poverty; you see Jesus alleviating poverty.

"Master, these people don't have anything to eat."

"Tell them to sit down, and we'll feed them."

"But we only have five loaves of bread and two fish."

He multiplied it so that 5,000 people ate until full, and full baskets were left over.

WAS JESUS WELL DRESSED?

The custom was to tear up the garments of those who were crucified. But when they saw Jesus' garment they said, *"Who is this man whose garment is from Bozrah that has no seam?"* They said, *"We're not ripping this up. I want it."* The other guy said, *"I want it."* They said, *"Let's gamble for it."*

They literally argued over who would take Jesus' garment because it was worth so much money. Seamless clothing is still highly valued today. You'd have to be a fool to believe Jesus was poor.

QUESTION 5

HOW DO YOU DEFINE PROSPERITY TO MAKE YOU HATE IT SO MUCH?

I want to know how someone defines prosperity to make them hate it.

People say, "I hate prosperity."

Really? How could they become so stupid? What happened to them? Why is their brain damaged? Who are they angry at that it's taken out on the prosperity message?

Bishop David Oyedepo defines prosperity as "God financially empowering you to meet the needs of a hurting world." I agree. Do you hate that? Imagine telling a lady, "Sorry to hear that your son just died and you don't have enough money to bury his body. All the best to you." What if you could pay for the funeral? What kind of person would hate that? That would be really stupid, selfish, and brain-damaged.

What's the definition of prosperity that makes people hate it so much?

Prosperity enables someone who had to spend two and a half hours a day riding a bus to rise up in the blessing of God so they can buy a car and be home with their kids for two and a half more hours each day.

Prosperity enables a mother to stay home and raise her children in the fear and admonition of the Lord rather than drop her children off at daycare or go to after-school programs, where her children are raised by the state from 8 a.m. to 5:30 p.m.

Some hate prosperity; I hate poverty. How can people not see?

I guarantee you that when everything that's been hidden is revealed on Judgment Day—many of the people who attacked prosperity preachers and the prosperity message will be exposed for receiving funding from people like George Soros. The world has a plan for you to live in lack, so you work endlessly for some faceless corporation while the public schools, before-school programs, and after-school programs get 10 hours a day with your children. You and your spouse get to see each other for 20 minutes a day—10 minutes in the morning, 10 minutes just before bed, too exhausted to speak to each other, and too exhausted to have sex, while the divorce rate keeps skyrocketing.

It's a wicked plan. If God hates prosperity and the Devil loves prosperity, how come the Egyptians didn't bless the Israelites? How come they put them to work 16 hours a day to destroy them and keep them from multiplying? When God delivered them, He said, *"Ask your captors for their silver and their gold. In this way will you plunder the Egyptians"* (Exodus 3:22). So-called ministers who oppose prosperity lie to people in church.

My wife and I recently went away for two weeks out in the middle of the beautiful desert in Arizona, on Navajo land much of the time, just to stare at the mountains and speak to each other. Do you think that weakened or strengthened our marriage? We came home the most in love and the closest we've been in 13 years of marriage. It takes money to do those things. Many couples would love to take a trip like that, but they either can't afford it or they aren't permitted vacation time from their jobs.

 Prosperity empowers people to bless their families and meet the needs of a hurting worl..

Do you think God wants people to rent from heathens who take the money and support planned parenthood or some other wicked thing? I want to know. I want an answer to my questions from those who hate the prosperity message. These people have identified themselves as wicked fools.

How do people define prosperity that causes them to hate it so much? My definition is: Prosperity empowers people to bless their families and meet the needs of a hurting world. Do you think that's of the Devil?

The Bible is clear on it.

QUESTION 6

IS POVERTY LISTED IN SCRIPTURE AS A BLESSING OR A CURSE?

We already read the blessing part. Let's read the curse part. Deuteronomy 28 will straighten out your doctrine. It lets you know what's from God and what comes into your life when you turn against God.

> *"But if you refuse to listen to the Lord your God and do not obey all the commands and decrees I am giving you today, all these curses will come and overwhelm you:"*
>
> — DEUTERONOMY 28:15

> *"You will plant much but harvest little, for locusts will eat your crops. You will plant vineyards and care for them, but you will not drink the wine or eat the grapes, for worms will destroy the vines. You will grow olive trees throughout your land, but you will never use the olive oil, for the fruit will drop before it ripens."*
>
> — DEUTERONOMY 28:38-40

"You will serve your enemies whom the Lord will send against you. You will be left hungry, thirsty, naked, and lacking in everything.

— DEUTERONOMY 28:48

Is poverty listed as a curse or a blessing? It's the curse of all curses. This chapter will straighten out your doctrine. It lets you know what's from God and what comes into your life if you turn against God. Without fully understanding this, your actions could unknowingly be shutting out the blessing and inviting the curse in. How? It's mentioned above, in Deuteronomy 28:15, that the key is to listen to God and all of the decrees that He's giving, and these are the curses that will follow. How many Christians know what the Bible says on this, thoroughly understanding the blessing and the curse as it is laid out here in the scriptures? Or do they simply just know the religious doctrine that's been repeated to them by their church or other Christians? Let your beliefs on prosperity be guided by what the Word of God has to say.

 Poverty is the curse of all curses.

Of all the curses listed from Deuteronomy 28:15 to the end of the chapter, poverty, scarcity, lack, hunger, nakedness, and working hard in vain (not being able to harvest the crops) is worse than any other curse, including sickness and disease. It gives a lot of examples of working hard—toiling without being able to prosper and fully reap the benefits of the hard labor. How many Christians do you know that are locked into 9–5 jobs, living from paycheck to paycheck, with little money left over for enjoyment? The Scripture above even says that they will *serve their enemies.* There are Christians working for corporations that are serving causes in opposition to their biblical values. These companies are actively looking to shut down the church and destroy the institution of family.

Is poverty named in scripture as a blessing or a curse? Poverty is clearly named in the Bible as a curse.

QUESTION 7

IF GOD LOVES POVERTY SO MUCH, WHY DID HE NEVER GIVE IT AS A REWARD?

If God supposedly loves poverty so much, why did He never once give it to anyone in the Bible as a reward for obedience? I want an answer. Where did God ever give poverty as a reward? But it can't be answered.

Those who hate prosperity have probably never thought about this once in their life. And yet, they convince people that poverty is desirable over prosperity, that it is more godly and honorable. The Kingdom of God has rewards. There are tangible rewards for serving God.

> *And it is impossible to please God without faith. Anyone who wants to come to him must believe that God exists and that he rewards those who sincerely seek him.*
>
> — HEBREWS 11:6

A wicked person earns deceptive wages,
   but the one who sows righteousness reaps a sure reward.

— PROVERBS 11:18 (NIV)

For those claiming that every reward or blessing from the Lord is "spiritual" and not referring to material wealth, it's interesting that the verse above is talking about wages or earned income. Spiritual blessings surely exist, but when people need help, God surely provides and He rewards people in visible ways.

Elijah didn't have to take the ravens to an Applebee's to pitch his vision and try to convince them to give! They just flew in with bread and meat twice a day. It was supernatural. That's what Jesus has done for my family. We have testimony after testimony of God's supernatural provision.

 There are rewards for serving God, and poverty is not one of them.

In the year 1990, I was at home with my mom while my dad was preaching in Germany. My mother had very little money and was about to sit down to pray about how she was going to make it through the weekend with no groceries. Before she could pray, there was a knock at the door. A lady smoking a cigarette (a complete stranger) handed my mother an envelope with $380 and then drove away. Back then, you could buy a lot of groceries for that amount. Meanwhile, my father was in Germany and had run out of money. He was walking on the street and felt a wind blow at his feet. Thinking it was leaves, he looked down and saw several bills in German money. These are just a few of the supernatural ways that God has shown up in the lives of my family members.

There are certainly rewards for serving God, and poverty is not one of them. If you make God's house a priority, God's blessing will visit your house. If you make God's family a priority (the church body), God will visit your family. If you make God's work a priority, God will visit your work.

QUESTION 8

WHAT DOES IT MEAN TO HAVE A CUP OF BLESSINGS THAT OVERFLOWS?

D o you celebrate an empty cup?

You prepare a feast for me
in the presence of my enemies.
You honor me by anointing my head with oil.
My cup overflows with blessings.

— PSALM 23:5

Explain what the Psalmist meant when he said in Psalm 23:5, *"My cup overflows with blessings."* What do you believe it means to have a cup of blessings that overflows?

The threshing floors will be filled with grain;
the vats will overflow with new wine and oil.

— JOEL 2:24 (NIV)

 An overflow to share with others.

...then your barns will be filled to overflowing,
and your vats will brim over with new wine.

— PROVERBS 3:10 (NIV)

A focal point of prosperity, consistent through God's Word, is over-flow. It is a Kingdom principle, impossible to escape. God does not expect you to give out of what you don't have or to give if you have nothing. He doesn't want you to have to choose between feeding your own children and feeding those in need. The concept of over-flow is having so much that after your own needs are met, there's enough to share with others.

May the Lord make your love increase and overflow for each other
and for everyone else, just as ours does for you.

— 1 THESSALONIANS 3:12 (NIV)

QUESTION 9

IF GOD LOVES POVERTY, HOW DO YOU
EXPLAIN ELIJAH AND ELISHA'S MINISTRY?

If God loves poverty and hates the abundance of material possessions, how do you explain Elijah's ministry and Elisha's ministry?

When Elijah found a widow, a single mother who was down to one meal, how come he didn't take her food and burn her house down? How come he did a miracle by the power of God to cause the cruse of oil to overflow and the jar of meal to never run out? Explain it. Was Elijah a witch? Was he a sorcerer, or was he a prophet of God? If poverty is of God, then he misused God's power, which you can't do without consequence.

Explain this...

> One day the widow of a member of the group of prophets came to
>   Elisha and cried out, "My husband who served you is dead, and
>   you know how he feared the Lord. But now a creditor has come,
>   threatening to take my two sons as slaves."
> "What can I do to help you?" Elisha asked. "Tell me, what do you
>   have in the house?"

"Nothing at all, except a flask of olive oil," she replied.

And Elisha said, "Borrow as many empty jars as you can from your friends and neighbors. Then go into your house with your sons and shut the door behind you. Pour olive oil from your flask into the jars, setting each one aside when it is filled."

So she did as she was told. Her sons kept bringing jars to her, and she filled one after another. Soon every container was full to the brim!

"Bring me another jar," she said to one of her sons.

"There aren't any more!" he told her. And then the olive oil stopped flowing.

When she told the man of God what had happened, he said to her, "Now sell the olive oil and pay your debts, and you and your sons can live on what is left over."

— 2 KINGS 4:1-7

Some people like to say, "God will never do anything for you that's just meant for you; it's meant for the Kingdom." —not true. That miracle was just to bless that woman and her sons. The resources supernaturally given to her were turned into wealth to both pay off debt and then to live comfortably from that point onward.

QUESTION 10

IF GOD LOVES POVERTY, WHY DID JESUS FEED THE MULTITUDE AND NEARLY SINK PETER'S BOAT?

I f God loves poverty and hates abundance, explain your thoughts on Christ feeding the multitude. Wouldn't hunger and lack have made them more holy?

> *Jesus said, "Have the people sit down." There was plenty of grass in that place, and they sat down (about five thousand men were there). Jesus then took the loaves, gave thanks, and distributed to those who were seated as much as they wanted. He did the same with the fish.*
> *When they had all had enough to eat, he said to his disciples, "Gather the pieces that are left over. Let nothing be wasted." So they gathered them and filled twelve baskets with the pieces of the five barley loaves left over by those who had eaten.*
>
> — JOHN 6:10-13 (NIV)

Then he said, "Throw out your net on the right-hand side of the boat, and you'll get some!" So they did, and they couldn't haul in the net because there were so many fish in it.

— JOHN 21: 6

Why did the Lord nearly sink Peter's boat with abundance? I'd love to hear the answer from those who hate prosperity. I know they don't have one. Additionally, why did God feed the multitude?

 Everyone ate until full.

The answer to both of these questions is essentially the same. God loves people and hates lack. It could be a lack of food, lack of money or resources. The day He fed the multitude, Jesus knew people would be traveling from far away. There were crowds of grown men, women, children, and babies. These were all people coming to hear Jesus teach. Can you see how the Lord's prosperity for them was a grand gesture to care for their needs? Think of when people plan a wedding or a large event. It takes so much money in order for each person to be fed. It's common to pay $100 per plate for each guest. How much in modern-day costs would that much fish and bread be worth? What a lavish God! When you understand that the Lord's actions are a part of who He is, you'll see that the Bible isn't just stories of old.

He is near to people's hearts and practical daily needs. In Peter's case, can you imagine the stress of staying up and working all night long without catching any fish? What was that worth to Peter to be alleviated of the burden when the overwhelming catch came in? Notice what He didn't do. Jesus didn't show up on the scene and say, "Well, all you need is me. Now that I'm here, my presence is enough."

It's foolish for people to think that's what Jesus is. No, instead, Jesus helped him solve the problem, and they were provided for.

QUESTION 11

DID CHRIST CONDEMN THE PRODUCTIVE SERVANT AND PRAISE THE ONE WHO BURIED THE MONEY?

When Jesus divided talents of gold to three servants in proportion to their abilities and then came back to get an account for what they did with it, did He rebuke the two who doubled their money? He didn't say, "Well, it was a test. I gave you money, and it was important to you, and you used it to double it. Now, I'm taking it from you, and I'm giving it to the one to whom it meant nothing." He buried it in the ground because if you're really spiritual, money won't matter to you.

> Now after a long time the master of those servants came and settled accounts with them. And he who had received the five talents came forward, bringing five talents more, saying, 'Master, you delivered to me five talents; here, I have made five talents more.' His master said to him, 'Well done, good and faithful servant. You have been faithful over a little; I will set you over much. Enter into the joy of your master.'
>
> — MATTHEW 25:19-21 (ESV)

No! In fact, He cursed the servant who took the money and buried it and rewarded the productive servants. That servant was actually referred to as "wicked" in another verse.

 He rewarded the productive servant.

How do you explain this? I'd love to hear the thoughts of those who oppose prosperity!

Many folks don't have any original thoughts because they've never actually thought about it; they just repeat what they've been told.

Furthermore, when it comes to money, people's mentalities are often not logical. There are ministers against prosperity who will decide to get a loan on their church building because they assume to themselves, "Where else are we going to get that kind of money?" Instead of believing God for the finances, they get a loan and then use the congregation's tithe money to pay down the interest. They end up paying above and beyond what the building is worth, and they use the congregation's tithes and offerings to do it. Meanwhile, they'll criticize a minister who can afford to pay cash for their church building. This is the opposite of what Jesus did; He wouldn't condemn the servant who is producing more and being faithful with the church's money.

They tell themselves, "People don't have that kind of money." The truth is that God has people who care about the Kingdom. Take, for instance, David from the Bible; he's one of those types of people. He produced to the point of being able to build the House of the Lord up with opulence.

*"With all my resources I have provided for the temple of my God—
gold for the gold work, silver for the silver, bronze for the bronze,
iron for the iron and wood for the wood, as well as onyx for the*

settings, turquoise, stones of various colors, and all kinds of fine stone and marble—all of these in large quantities. Besides, in my devotion to the temple of my God I now give my personal treasures of gold and silver for the temple of my God, over and above everything I have provided for this holy temple."

— 1 CHRONICLES 29: 2, 3 (NIV)

When you don't allow God's people an opportunity to give (especially on a Kingdom advancement project), you rob them of the opportunity to engage in the same act as the servants who multiplied the talents. It's not good for a minister to assume that "no one has the money" or that people don't want to be a part of giving. There are, in fact, people who produce faithfully and are rewarded for it by the Lord. It's interesting how productive believers receive backlash from others for doing so.

QUESTION 12

HOW CAN SOMEONE BE THE LENDER AND NEVER THE BORROWER?

I f you think God just wants your basic needs supplied, how does this Scripture make sense to you?

> *"The LORD will send rain at the proper time from his rich treasury in the heavens and will bless all the work you do. You will lend to many nations, but you will never need to borrow from them."*
>
> — DEUTERONOMY 28:12

God said, *"You will lend to many nations, but you will never need to borrow from them."*

People against prosperity probably think God is happy when a Christian finances a car for six years at 11 percent interest with a company that takes advantage of poor people who can't afford cars. I'm sure some think that's the plan of God.

 Can a poor person lend and never borrow?

How does a poor person lend and never borrow? They can't! Many Christians are living the opposite of the Biblical standard of being the lender. They are borrowing—they have just as many loans and debts as the next person. They do not realize how much more they are paying for some of these items and how that extra money could be used to advance themselves and the Kingdom of God.

They are so used to being the borrower they didn't consider that there are other options. As stated before, there are spiritual powers of darkness at play here, causing people to be blinded. The controversial subject of prosperity is one that draws the anger of Hell more than any other subject. When you deal with prosperity, you touch on the money system of the world. This is what the god of mammon controls.

Jesse Duplantis teaches about prosperity, and many hate him for it. The spiritual reason for that is because he's teaching people how to buck the world's control and bypass the whole demonic system by entering into the blessing of God. Sometimes, when I begin teaching on this topic, people suspiciously say, "That sounds like that prosperity message." People act as if that's not in the Bible, as though prosperity is some type of infectious disease. Is this in the Bible or not? Does Biblical prosperity include being the lender and not the borrower? Yes, it does!

QUESTION 13

HOW CAN A RIGHTEOUS MAN LEAVE AN INHERITANCE TO HIS CHILDREN'S CHILDREN?

How can a righteous man leave an inheritance to his children's children when you believe wealth is wicked and poverty is righteous?

> *Trouble chases sinners,*
> *while blessings reward the righteous.*
> *Good people leave an inheritance to their grandchildren,*
> *but the sinner's wealth passes to the godly.*
>
> — PROVERBS 13:21, 22

What does it mean that there's a spiritual law that the wealth of the wicked passes to the godly?

I would love to hear your answer.

Even the rudimentary requirements of Christianity need an overflow of finances. Feeding the hungry, clothing the naked, taking care of widows and orphans, giving to the Lord at least 10 percent (for the tithe), and leaving an inheritance to your children's children. Religion binds people to the point that they don't grasp all these scriptural commands. They think of the word "money," and their mind immediately jumps to "evil." In reality, that religious mindset is blocking them from obeying large portions of Scripture.

> *Anyone who does not provide for their relatives, and especially for their own household, has denied the faith and is worse than an unbeliever.*
>
> — 1 TIMOTHY 5:8 (NIV)

It actually takes finances to fulfill the requirements of Scripture.

 It's more than a spiritual inheritance.

I don't think people realize the seriousness of what the Bible requires of us. Many Christians are so accustomed to the ways of this world, and they know so little of their Bible that their mindset is secular instead of scriptural.

QUESTION 14

IF YOU BELIEVE MONEY IS EVIL, WHY DO YOU CARRY ANY?

I don't allow wicked things in my house. I believe pornography is evil; I don't keep a little in my house. There's no alcohol in my house, not even a little.

Anything the Bible says is evil or wicked must be removed from your life, not just lessened. If you truly believe money is wicked, why do you carry any? Are you a hypocrite?

If money is evil, you have some explaining to do if you enclose it in a child's birthday card. You don't give a child a little liquor, and you don't give a child a little bit of pornography because both are evil.

 If money is evil, why do you have it in your pocket?

If you give something as a gift that you consider evil, then you're evil.

Dear friends, this is now my second letter to you. I have written both of them as reminders to stimulate you to wholesome thinking.

— 2 PETER 3:1 (NIV)

It's amazing how the enemy has twisted and perverted the prosperity of God to be interpreted as evil. Still today, believers need to be guided and encouraged in their thinking.

Romans 12:9 says, *Hate what is wrong. Hold tightly to what is good.*

The crux of prosperity is that there are people on their way to Hell because they've never heard the gospel, and they can't hear it unless someone tells them.

When I hear Christians say that they don't care about prosperity, all I can hear them saying is that they don't care about the lost being saved (souls won for the Kingdom). Anybody with a brain understands that it takes money to win souls. The more money you have, the more souls you can win. That's why it's important not to confuse what is evil with what is good.

QUESTION 15

DO YOU NOT UNDERSTAND THAT PROSPERITY AND SUFFERING CAN COEXIST?

Y ou whine about prosperity preachers teaching that if you serve God, He'll bless you with material things when the Bible talks about suffering resulting from serving the Lord.

You can have more than one thing. Prosperity and suffering are not mutually exclusive.

> When Isaac planted his crops that year, he harvested a hundred
> times more grain than he planted, for the Lord blessed him. He
> became a very rich man, and his wealth continued to grow. He
> acquired so many flocks of sheep and goats, herds of cattle, and
> servants that the Philistines became jealous of him. So the
> Philistines filled up all of Isaac's wells with dirt. These were the
> wells that had been dug by the servants of his father, Abraham.
> Finally, Abimelech ordered Isaac to leave the country. "Go some-
> where else," he said, "for you have become too powerful for us."
> So Isaac moved away to the Gerar Valley, where he set up their tents
> and settled down. He reopened the wells his father had dug,

which the Philistines had filled in after Abraham's death. Isaac
also restored the names Abraham had given them.

Isaac's servants also dug in the Gerar Valley and discovered a well
of fresh water. But then the shepherds from Gerar came and
claimed the spring. "This is our water," they said, and they
argued over it with Isaac's herdsmen. So Isaac named the well
Esek (which means "argument"). Isaac's men then dug another
well, but again there was a dispute over it. So Isaac named it
Sitnah (which means "hostility"). Abandoning that one, Isaac
moved on and dug another well. This time there was no dispute
over it, so Isaac named the place Rehoboth (which means "open
space"), for he said, "At last the Lord has created enough space
for us to prosper in this land."

— GENESIS 26:12-22

We observe from the above passage that the blessing of the Lord
didn't bring poverty to Isaac. Instead, it multiplied what he was
doing. It says plainly that he became a *very rich* man and that his
wealth continued to grow. The Philistines envied him and then started
disputes with him when he began using the original wells that his
father dug. Notice the only people that gave Isaac a hard time for
prospering were his enemies. Those who give others a hard time
because they are prospering are enemies of the church. I personally
wouldn't trust anyone who felt that the church shouldn't be blessed
or that Christians shouldn't be blessed. As you can see, he suffered
through the way he was treated, yet at the same time, he was financially blessed.

 You can have both at the same time.

One of the huge doctrinal mistakes people make is thinking there
can only be one thing or another.

"Well, these guys teach prosperity, but the Bible said there'd be suffering if you serve the Lord."

You can actually have both. Jesus taught both in the same portion of Scripture.

Mark 10, beginning in verse 28, Jesus was traveling with His disciples, and Peter began to speak up and tell about everything they had given up to follow Christ.

> "Yes," Jesus replied, "and I assure you that everyone who has given
> up house or brothers or sisters or mother or father or children or
> property, for my sake and for the Good News, will receive now
> in return a hundred times as many houses, brothers, sisters,
> mothers, children, and property—along with persecution. And in
> the world to come that person will have eternal life."
>
> — MARK 10: 29, 30

Jesus said, "Yes. Anyone that gives up property or possession among other things will receive now and in this life property, possessions, and houses along with persecution." So they go together.

No one who understands the Bible teaches that you won't have troubles if you serve the Lord.

> "I have told you these things, so that in Me you may have [perfect]
> peace and confidence. In the world you have tribulation and tri-
> als and distress and frustration; but be of good cheer [take
> courage; be confident, certain, undaunted]! For I have overcome
> the world. [I have deprived it of power to harm you and have
> conquered it for you.]"
>
> — JOHN 16:33 (AMPC)

Do you not understand that prosperity and suffering can coexist? If not, you've never read about the life of Isaac.

You don't choose one or the other. It's not all suffering, and it's not all prosperity with no opposition. As you increase, just like with Isaac, the Devil looks to shut you down, but God gives you power, as He did in the early church. You can put Paul in prison, but good luck keeping him there. You can put Peter in prison, but good luck keeping him there.

QUESTION 16

IS IT HYPOCRITICAL TO SPEAK AGAINST PROSPERITY WHILE ENJOYING LAVISH AMERICAN LUXURY?

When I hear an American criticize the prosperity message, I know I'm listening to a liar and a hypocrite. I won't call them out by name because I'm not against people. I'm for people, even enemies, even people that hate me.

As someone with a father who's been in the ministry for 40 years and myself for over 17 years, people who criticize the prosperity message often live better materially than the preachers they criticize —they just hide it.

Do you think it's hypocritical to write a book, bash prosperity, and earn a million dollars from it? I would feel like a hypocrite.

You say, "I don't believe in prosperity."

 You're already living in prosperity.

The average person on planet Earth drives an ox cart. That's a fact. For you to live in America, Europe, or Canada and say you don't believe in prosperity is absurd. I'd like to see your house. I'd like to know if you have electricity and air conditioning. I'd love to see whether you walk or ride a bicycle. The next person I meet who attacks prosperity while living in poverty as they preach will be the first one I've ever met.

"Well, Jesus didn't drive a Cadillac."

He didn't drive a Ford or have a truck, either.

If you believe what you tell others, you should be riding a donkey to church on Sunday. Jesus used the best transportation of His day. Because He has a well-functioning brain, He would do the same thing today. If there's a mode of transportation that can get you somewhere in 50 minutes and another mode of transportation that takes 30 hours, you don't have to pray about which one to use.

"Jesus didn't drive a nice car."

He didn't drive a bad car, like the one you have, either—you're still a hypocrite.

QUESTION 17

DO YOU BELIEVE THE BLESSING OF ABRAHAM IS NOT FOR CHRISTIANS AND DOESN'T INCLUDE FINANCIAL WEALTH?

I n some ways, many lower-income Americans live better than John Rockefeller lived as a billionaire. For instance, John Rockefeller didn't have air conditioning—he sweated in the summer in his own home.

Look at how the rest of the world lives and realize you're living in prosperity, whether or not you think you are. Who do you think gave you prosperity? Do you think the Devil gave you your home? Do you think the Devil gave you air conditioning and food?

> In the same way, "Abraham believed God, and God counted him as
> righteous because of his faith." The real children of Abraham,
> then, are those who put their faith in God.
> What's more, the Scriptures looked forward to this time when God
> would make the Gentiles right in his sight because of their faith.
> God proclaimed this good news to Abraham long ago when he
> said, "All nations will be blessed through you." So all who put

their faith in Christ share the same blessing Abraham received because of his faith.

— GALATIANS 3:6-9

 Everyone who puts their faith in Christ shares the same blessing Abraham received because of his faith.

We already covered Abraham's story earlier. Scripture tells us that he was *very rich and increased in cattle, silver, and gold.* On a different note, remember the curse from Deuteronomy 28? Take a look at what happened to the curse in the passage below:

But Christ has rescued us from the curse pronounced by the law. When he was hung on the cross, he took upon himself the curse for our wrongdoing. For it is written in the Scriptures, "Cursed is everyone who is hung on a tree." Through Christ Jesus, God has blessed the Gentiles with the same blessing he promised to Abraham, so that we who are believers might receive the promised Holy Spirit through faith.

— GALATIANS 3:13, 14

And now that you belong to Christ, you are the true children of Abraham. You are his heirs, and God's promise to Abraham belongs to you.

— GALATIANS 3:29

QUESTION 18

DOES GOOD STEWARDSHIP NOT LEAD TO AN INCREASE?

I f you think good stewardship leads to a financial decrease, then you should remove the entire book of Proverbs from your Bible.

Wisdom leads to wealth. Proper management leads to wealth. That's a Bible principle.

If you are a good steward of what God gives you, increase follows. This is not a difficult concept to understand, yet somehow, many ministers and Christians get tripped up on this.

When I came out of Bible college, I was on fire for the Lord. I wanted to get the whole world saved—many new ministers are like that. When they first come out of Bible school they are excited, and their passion for the Kingdom of God is on fire. The first major obstacle they hit is the lack of financial resources needed to do the ministry they desire. When facing this economic reality, they have three possible choices. The first option is to quit. The second choice is to alter their vision and lower their dreams. The third and hardest option is to press in and receive revelation from God. When this test happens, it's important to be faithful in handling the harvest that comes in.

 The more faithful you are in handling what you have, the more you will be given.

The truth is, I was not ready to steward large amounts of money at the time I graduated from college. As you can guess, the first and the second options were not the path I took. I took the third option; I pressed in and received revelation from God. As you faithfully steward what He's given you, you gradually rise to new levels. God will give you more when He knows He can trust you.

When you start thinking strategically about how many people you would like to bring to the Lord, God will give you strategies to make this a reality. You may think about how many salvations you would like to see for the year in your ministry or ask yourself what it would take to bring 1000 new people to faith in Christ. Just about every idea or plan God gives you will involve money. This is true, especially when you desire to reach large numbers of people. Money amplifies the gospel. When you have money, you can rent out a stadium and pay to advertise on 100 billboards. You can do bigger things for the Kingdom. The more faithful you are with what you have, the more you will be given.

QUESTION 19

HOW DO YOU EXPLAIN THE EARLY CHURCH HAVING POVERTY TOTALLY ERADICATED AFTER THEY GAVE?

How do you explain the early church having poverty totally eradicated after they gave? If you say that you hate the prosperity message, I want to hear your explanation.

"Well, the early church was poor."

Were they?

> All the believers were united in heart and mind. And they felt that what they owned was not their own, so they shared everything they had. The apostles testified powerfully to the resurrection of the Lord Jesus, and God's great blessing was upon them all. There were no needy people among them, because those who owned land or houses would sell them and bring the money to the apostles to give to those in need.

For instance, there was Joseph, the one the apostles nicknamed Barnabas (which means "Son of Encouragement"). He was from the tribe of Levi and came from the island of Cyprus. He sold a field he owned and brought the money to the apostles.

— ACTS 4:32-37

It clearly explains here in the Scriptures that poverty was eradicated from the early church. I wish people would read the Bible and quit repeating clichés like, "Well, the early church was very poor." That's not what it says in the above text. It actually says, "There weren't any poor people among them."

 There were no poor among them.

When you give in obedience to what the Lord is directing you to do, it puts you in the flow of the Holy Ghost. The Bible says to *seek first the Kingdom of God, and all else will be added.* The early church definitely moved in that flow. They heard from God regarding the needs of others and acted in faith to meet those needs. Because of this, they experienced supernatural provision; therefore, no one was in lack.

QUESTION 20

DOES GOD WANT THE WORLD'S WEALTH CONTROLLED BY THE WICKED?

D oes God want the world's wealth controlled by the wicked so they can use it to rule over the righteous? I would love to hear your answer.

Money is not just going to lie idly in the streets. So, if the Church rejects money and says, "No, money is not important to us."—the money that exists will be taken by wicked people.

Christians don't realize that if money is not important to them, then other people and their needs are not important to them. If money is not important to Christians, then helping the poor, orphans, and widows is not important to them.

 When money is no longer recognized by believers as a valuable resource, it flows to wicked people and is used for wicked purposes.

The more money a truly righteous man has, the better off the world is. The less money the righteous have, the worse off the world is.

The Bible says in Proverbs 22:7, *The rich rule over the poor.*

Given this, do you believe God wants the wealth of the world controlled by the wicked so that they can rule over the righteous? I would love to hear your answer because according to what you believe, that's what will happen. When Christians believe they shouldn't want wealth, the wicked will take it and use it against the church. *The wealth of the wicked is laid up for the just.*

> *So even though wisdom is better than strength, those who are wise will be despised if they are poor. What they say will not be appreciated for long.*
>
> — ECCLESIASTES 9:16

Have you considered that the reason there are powers working to keep the church poor and influencing Christians to disdain wealth is to keep our voices from being heard?

People who are against prosperity: Do you like the fact that there are more pay-per-view pornography channels than gospel preaching channels? Until you receive a revelation on this, the majority culture of evil will not bother you.

QUESTION 21

DOES WICKEDNESS CARRY A FINANCIAL BLESSING AND HOLINESS A FINANCIAL CURSE?

D oes wickedness carry a financial blessing and holiness a financial curse? Tell me.

You hate prosperity so much that you say, "These people teach that if you serve God, God will bless you with material things."

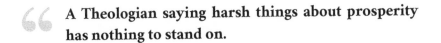

> **A Theologian saying harsh things about prosperity has nothing to stand on.**

You believe that if you live holy and obey God, He'll reward you with poverty—although it's not anywhere in the Bible—and there's actually a financial blessing for serving the Devil. Is that your belief?

Unfortunately, for you, the Bible says the opposite.

Oh, the joys of those who do not
follow the advice of the wicked,
or stand around with sinners,
or join in with mockers.

But they delight in the law of the Lord,
meditating on it day and night.
They are like trees planted along the riverbank,
bearing fruit each season.
Their leaves never wither,
and they prosper in all they do.
But not the wicked!
They are like worthless chaff, scattered by the wind.
They will be condemned at the time of judgment.
Sinners will have no place among the godly.
For the Lord watches over the path of the godly,
but the path of the wicked leads to destruction.

— PSALM 1:1-6

Do you believe that wickedness carries a financial blessing and holiness brings a financial curse? If you do, you're out of line with the Bible.

QUESTION 22

IS IT POSSIBLE TO HELP THE POOR, CLOTHE THE NAKED, AND FEED THE HUNGRY WHILE BEING POOR?

I s it possible to help the poor, clothe the naked, and feed the hungry while being poor? Do you believe it's possible? I'm asking you.

Do you believe it's possible to honor the commandments of Christ to help the poor, clothe the naked, feed the hungry, et cetera, while suffering from poverty yourself? If you do, you're wrong, according to the Bible, which is all I care about.

> *Whoever gives to the poor will lack nothing,*
> *but those who close their eyes to poverty will be cursed.*

> — PROVERBS 28:27

> *Oh, the joys of those who are kind to the poor!*
> *The Lord rescues them when they are in trouble.*
> *The Lord protects them*
> *and keeps them alive.*
> *He gives them prosperity in the land*

and rescues them from their enemies.
The Lord nurses them when they are sick
and restores them to health.

— PSALM 41:1-3

Anytime you talk about prosperity, the bitter people say, "Why don't those preachers sell what they have and give it to the poor?"

Why don't you try it sometime? I've already done it. The money keeps boomeranging back.

I was sitting next to a drunk lady on an airplane in first class. She rambled on for two hours and had four glasses of champagne. Two or three hours passed until she asked, "What do you do for a living?"

"I'm a minister."

"A minister?" almost spitting out her champagne. "A minister sitting in first class?"

I should have told her I was an assassin, a pornographer, an adulterous movie star, a brewery owner, or anyone whom the world accepts as worthy of having money.

It's okay to sit in first class—except for people who serve the Lord.

"A preacher sitting in first class, I thought you people were supposed to give all your money to the poor."

I told that woman, "I tried to give all my money to the poor. The more I gave, the more it multiplied back."

Actually, I struggled in life when I had no plan to help the poor. I was so focused on my poverty that I didn't look to help other people. I just looked for people to help me. When I went to a nation and dealt with poverty for the first time—real poverty—and saw how some of my brothers and sisters in Christ lived in other countries, it broke my heart. I was in a slum in another country and met women whose babies were crying because they didn't have any food. The mother couldn't give them any food because she hadn't eaten. Her breasts weren't producing milk. I'd never seen anything like that before.

I held it together for the day. But when I returned to my hotel, I cried till about five in the morning. I felt the Lord speak to me, "You've done something good today. Do you want to make that a one-day thing, or do you want to do that continually?" I didn't even answer the question. I just called Adalis, and we made a pledge to Feed the Hungry for an amount that was more than what we were paying to rent our apartment, like $800 a month. I figured in the worst-case scenario, I'd lose my apartment. But I would rather live in my car with my wife than not do something about what I'd seen.

Well, what happened? Did I lose my apartment? Nope. Everything increased. Money started coming in from seemingly everywhere. I did something wise. I upped the amount from 40 kids a day to 80 kids a day. I experienced more increases, so I upped it to 200. More money came in. I upped it to 800, and now it's a thousand children a day.

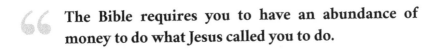

The Bible requires you to have an abundance of money to do what Jesus called you to do.

Whenever you hear someone criticize the prosperity message and say, "How come these guys don't sell their jets and give the money to the poor?" do you ever think that the reason they got a jet is by considering the poor? Money doesn't work the way you think it does. When you give, you receive. *Pressed down, shaken together, and running over. I will cause men to give liberally and bountifully into your bosom.* (Luke 6:38)

Do you believe it's possible to honor the commitments of Christ while being impoverished yourself? The Bible requires you to have an abundance of money to do what Jesus called you to do. How can you feed the hungry and clothe the naked when you're in lack? You can't help the needy when you're needy. You can't help the poor when you're one of them. So, the basic requirements of Christ cause you to rise out of poverty into abundance.

QUESTION 23

IF A PERSON GAVE ALL THEIR MONEY TO THE POOR, WHAT WOULD HAPPEN TO THEM?

N otice the blessings the Bible says come to those who give go beyond money.

Oh, the joys of those who are kind to the poor!
The Lord rescues them when they are in trouble.
The Lord protects them
and keeps them alive.
He gives them prosperity in the land
and rescues them from their enemies.
The Lord nurses them when they are sick
and restores them to health.

— PSALM 41:1-3

Yes, God will multiply your resources, but it extends beyond that. If a person gave all their money to the poor, what would happen to them? Those who give to the poor are actually lending to the Lord.

In Caesarea there lived a Roman army officer named Cornelius, who was a captain of the Italian Regiment. He was a devout, God-fearing man, as was everyone in his household. He gave generously to the poor and prayed regularly to God. One afternoon about three o'clock, he had a vision in which he saw an angel of God coming toward him. "Cornelius!" the angel said.
Cornelius stared at him in terror. "What is it, sir?" he asked the angel.
And the angel replied, "Your prayers and gifts to the poor have been received by God as an offering! Now send some men to Joppa, and summon a man named Simon Peter. He is staying with Simon, a tanner who lives near the seashore."

— ACTS 10:1-6

Peter went to the home of Cornelius. Salvation and the baptism of the Holy Ghost came to his whole family.

You could never exhaust the far-reaching blessings that come to givers. That's why we always present an opportunity to give and don't do it in a typical donation style.

 I don't make donations. I sow seed.

We teach from the Bible that you're to give with an expectation of a supernatural harvest.

Separate yourself from the pack by being a giver. The Lord will keep you alive, protect you from your enemies, nurse you when you're sick, cause you to prosper in the land, and mobilize angels to get the gospel to your family. You provoke a blessing for your family. You're not helping God do His work. You are planting seeds in good soil, which will then produce a harvest for you.

QUESTION 24

DO YOU BELIEVE NO RICH MEN WILL BE IN HEAVEN?

D o you believe that there will be no rich men in Heaven? The biggest counterargument people have to this is the following: Jesus said, *"It's easier for a camel to get through the eye of a needle than it is for a rich man to enter the kingdom of heaven!"* (Matthew 19:24). He said that.

Do you think He meant the literal eye of a needle, like a sewing needle? That it's easier for a camel to go through that?

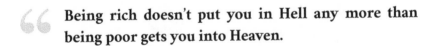

Being rich doesn't put you in Hell any more than being poor gets you into Heaven.

The eye of a needle was a gate in that land. It was a tiny gate and very narrow. The richer the man, the more he had to unload his possessions and the more time it took to go through the eye of the needle. If you think that's a verse that means no rich people are in Heaven, then Abraham is in Hell, Isaac is in Hell, Jacob is in Hell, Ruth and Boaz are in Hell, and David is in Hell.

Let's not forget that Jesus himself was wealthy, so why would He set that example without it being obtainable? How stupid can people be?

Being rich doesn't put you in Hell any more than being poor gets you into Heaven. You become saved when you're born again, regardless of financial status.

QUESTION 25

WHAT'S GOOD ABOUT THE CHURCH HAVING LESS MONEY?

You say, "I don't believe in prosperity."

Tell me something that's good about the church having less money. Who gives in church offerings, wicked people or righteous people?

 Less money means less impact. More money means more impact.

The more money the church has, the greater the impact it can make. The less money the church has, the less impact it makes.

It seems like the powers that control the propaganda news on CNN, NBC, and everywhere else know this truth. They want the church to disdain wealth so that they can't rise in power and do what God has called them to do.

So, what's good about the church having less money? Anything?

There are certain questions that common people don't ask. For example, when CNN does an exposé on a pastor who owns a jet, viewers don't ask themselves intelligent questions like, "How was that money obtained?" If obtained illegally, then there should be consequences. If the funds were acquired legally, the minister should be left alone. If something is legal to own, then anyone can own it. This is not a communist country. I've heard people argue, "Yeah, but they're a church. They don't pay taxes." My response is neither does the Red Cross. The Red Cross has planes—multiple planes! So why is it that you never see an exposé on casino owners, Hollywood stars, or producers? Jeffrey Epstein was using jets to fly pedophiles to his own private island to rape children. Then, a preacher comes along and people ask why a preacher needs a jet. The answer is to fly—the same reason every other person uses one.

I hear people say all the time regarding preachers, "They don't need a jet." How do people get to decide when or if someone is allowed to have something? What do you want them to do instead? Should they sail and then, six months later, arrive with rickets and scurvy? Why is it okay for everyone to become wealthy except for Christians? Why is it okay for every other group of people, but then when a Christian rises up into wealth, they are discriminated against? Most of the people who make these accusations and comments are not doing anything productive for the Kingdom of God or humanity. So you (as the reader) have a choice: to be a commenter or a doer. You can be somebody who makes an impact in life or someone who criticizes others who are doers.

QUESTION 26

ARE OFFERINGS IN THE BIBLE, OR ARE THEY A PERVERSION OF GOD'S WORD?

A re offerings actually in the Bible, or have they been invented by so-called prosperity preachers? Are offerings a perversion of the Word of God? I can teach for two hours on Bible prophecy, salvation, Heaven, and Hell, then take six minutes at the end of a broadcast to receive an offering for our ministry. What do people focus on?

"That's how I know he's not a man of God. If he was a man of God, he wouldn't talk about money."

It's interesting to me because it forces the following questions:

Are offerings not in the Bible?
Was the offering not instituted by God?
Are offerings a perversion of Scripture by people who don't know the Scriptures?

What's really true? Are offerings in the Bible, or are they a perversion of God's Word?

The first murder was over an offering.

Offerings stem back to the beginning of Genesis, when Abel brought an offering that pleased God, and Cain brought one but didn't please God.

Before sin came into the world, God reserved two trees that man couldn't touch.

Job brought offerings; Abraham paid a tithe. Later, it was instituted in the law that no man shall appear before the Lord without an offering; it was a central part of worship. Did you know that's in the Bible?

Did Jesus receive offerings, or did He tell everybody to give everything to the poor? A lady took perfume that was worth more than a year's wages and dumped it on His feet. Jesus didn't ask, "What are you doing? What a waste of money." It was the religious people who freaked out over money. As you can see, nothing's changed.

"That could have been sold and given to the poor."

Jesus responded, saying, *"Chill out. She did this to bless me, prepare me for my burial, and the story of what this woman has done will be told all over the world."*

Jesus received an offering that blessed Him personally. It wasn't even for His ministry, just for Him.

Did Jesus speak about offerings?

> *Give, and it shall be given unto you; good measure, pressed down, and shaken together, and running over, shall men give into your bosom. For with the same measure that ye mete withal it shall be measured to you again.*

> — LUKE 6:38 (KJV)

"Well, these preachers teach that if you give to God, He'll return back to you blessings." Do you know who started that teaching? Actually, He didn't start it. He echoed it—Jesus Christ said that.

Give, and it shall be given unto you... Notice that it doesn't say, "Do not give, and I'll receive."

I heard someone say, "I believe that we're not meant to walk in poverty, but there are many preachers that tickle the ears of the congregation in order to fill seats."

What does that have to do with anything? If every preacher who preached a prosperity message fell into sin today, how does that change anything that's in the Bible? Get your eyes off man and get your eyes on Christ and the Word. When a salvation preacher falls, do we all quit preaching salvation? Do what the Bible says.

Looking unto Jesus the author and finisher of our faith; who for the joy that was set before him endured the cross, despising the shame, and is set down at the right hand of the throne of God.

— HEBREWS 12:2 (KJV)

"There are so many people who preach prosperity. We don't need any more prosperity preachers."

Out of those who complain, they wouldn't be able to name ten preachers in the United States and Canada who preach prosperity, and you can throw Europe in, too. Tell me the names of all the people who preach prosperity. I enjoy listening to prosperity preaching. I can barely find anybody. I don't think I could name ten. Very few preach it. You need to go back and watch videos from the seventies and eighties. The people preaching it in the seventies and eighties don't preach it anymore. You can barely name any healing preachers anymore. Most backed away from teaching prosperity and healing because of criticism.

> *"Give, and you will receive. Your gift will return to you in full—pressed down, shaken together to make room for more, running over, and poured into your lap. The amount you give will determine the amount you get back."*
>
> — LUKE 6:38

"The measure you use in giving will determine the measure that comes back to you." This was not invented in America. Did Jesus say this at a faith convention in Tulsa?

Jesus said, *Give, and you shall receive, and the amount you use in giving is what determines what comes back to you.* So if Jesus was on Earth today, with a different name, they would group Him in with all the other people that religious people hate, and try to crucify Him again.

When I started understanding prosperity, my father told me, "Jonathan, just so you know, you're starting to get a reputation as a prosperity preacher."

I told him, "Tell everyone it's worse than what they heard." I'm not ashamed to have prosperity any more than I'm ashamed to be healed or forgiven or anything else that Jesus paid for with His blood. How about you?

> *Now I want you to know, dear brothers and sisters, what God in his kindness has done through the churches in Macedonia. They are being tested by many troubles, and they are very poor. But they are also filled with abundant joy, which has overflowed in rich generosity.*
> *For I can testify that they gave not only what they could afford, but*

*far more. And they did it of their own free will. They begged us
again and again for the privilege of sharing in the gift for the
believers in Jerusalem. They even did more than we had hoped,
for their first action was to give themselves to the Lord and to us,
just as God wanted them to do.*

*So we have urged Titus, who encouraged your giving in the first
place, to return to you and encourage you to finish this ministry
of giving.*

— 2 CORINTHIANS 8:1-6

*You know the generous grace of our Lord Jesus Christ. Though he
was rich, yet for your sakes he became poor, so that by his
poverty he could make you rich.*

— 2 CORINTHIANS 8:9

*And herein I give my advice: for this is expedient for you, who have
begun before, not only to do, but also to be forward a year ago.*

*Now therefore perform the doing of it; that as there was a readiness
to will, so there may be a performance also out of that which ye
have.*

*For if there be first a willing mind, it is accepted according to that a
man hath, and not according to that he hath not.*

— 2 CORINTHIANS 8:10-12 (KJV)

Paul sent a man named Titus for the sole purpose of encouraging the
cheapskate, immoral, Corinthian church to excel in the ministry of
giving.

Maybe you're thinking, "I don't see anywhere in the Bible where
someone was called just to take an offering."

How about Elijah? How about Titus? I'm sorry that you bought a discounted Bible with missing pages. It's right there; people are blind while claiming they can see.

> *But this I say, He which soweth sparingly shall reap also sparingly;*
> *and he which soweth bountifully shall reap also bountifully.*
> *Every man according as he purposeth in his heart, so let him give;*
> *not grudgingly, or of necessity: for God loveth a cheerful giver.*

> — 2 CORINTHIANS 9:6, 7 (KJV)

Incredibly, God instituted offerings, yet you are critical of receiving offerings. Meanwhile, no one bats an eye if you sell tickets to hear someone preach—something explicitly condemned in the Bible. Why? You'd think there'd be an uprising over such duplicity!

People are bombarded with so-called supernatural events or conferences via social media and the telephone. If you register now, you get a discount. If you miss the early registration, you must pay the full price. Where's that in the Bible?

You will give me heat because I do what Jesus said to do. Why? Because the Devil encourages people to accomplish things the world's way. There's no harvest for buying tickets; there's a harvest for giving as you're led by the Spirit. Jesus said, when you give, you will receive; buying a ticket is not giving. That's the exact opposite of what Paul talked about in 2 Corinthians 9. Purchasing a ticket is compulsory—that's forced giving; that's what they do at baseball games, football games, and now Christian conferences.

There was an anti-prosperity conference in Southern California that required the purchase of a ticket to attend. You weren't allowed in if you didn't pay. How come no one gave them a hard time?

Faith preachers, prosperity preachers—genuine ones—charge no fee to hear the gospel. They receive an offering at the end of the meeting for anyone who wants to give—it's a freewill offering. The Devil hates this because if a person gives, they will also receive. God instituted the offering to break the church out of poverty and swim in the abundance of God. It's in the Bible. Now, if you don't believe the Bible, I can't help you. Don't claim to believe the Bible and then talk about prosperity like it's not in the Bible—you have brain damage if you do. It's throughout the Bible. They took offerings in the garden. Adam's family gave offerings. Abraham gave, Isaac gave, Jacob gave. It ticked God off in Malachi because people weren't giving.

> *"I am the Lord, and I do not change. That is why you descendants of*
> *Jacob are not already destroyed. Ever since the days of your*
> *ancestors, you have scorned my decrees and failed to obey them.*
> *Now return to me, and I will return to you," says the Lord of*
> *Heaven's Armies.*
> *"But you ask, 'How can we return when we have never gone away?'*
> *"Should people cheat God? Yet you have cheated me!*
> *"But you ask, 'What do you mean? When did we ever cheat you?'*
> *"You have cheated me of the tithes and offerings due to me. You are*
> *under a curse, for your whole nation has been cheating me."*
>
> — MALACHI 3:6-9

God said there was a curse for not giving. Prosperity preachers didn't say that—God said that.

People hate the prosperity message because they hate hearing that money is a god in their life that they must sacrifice on the altar to have a relationship with God. You will never meet a giver who hates the message of prosperity.

When people obey the Bible regarding tithes, offerings, giving, and receiving, it changes their lives. It changed my life—turned my life around.

The Bible doesn't command preachers to only preach the gospel of Jesus Christ. It says to preach the whole counsel of God's Word—the entire thing, not just Christ. The gospel is preached to sinners, and the whole counsel of the Word of God to Christians—this includes giving.

> "Bring all the tithes into the storehouse so there will be enough food in my Temple. If you do," says the Lord of Heaven's Armies, "I will open the windows of heaven for you. I will pour out a blessing so great you won't have enough room to take it in! Try it! Put me to the test!"
>
> — MALACHI 3:10

Are modern prosperity preachers preaching strong on offerings? They actually go easy on people—too easy.

> The Lord of Heaven's Armies says to the priests: "A son honors his father, and a servant respects his master. If I am your father and master, where are the honor and respect I deserve? You have shown contempt for my name!
> "But you ask, 'How have we ever shown contempt for your name?'
> "You have shown contempt by offering defiled sacrifices on my altar.
> "Then you ask, 'How have we defiled the sacrifices?'
> "You defile them by saying the altar of the Lord deserves no respect. When you give blind animals as sacrifices, isn't that wrong? And isn't it wrong to offer animals that are crippled and diseased? Try giving gifts like that to your governor, and see how pleased he is!" says the Lord of Heaven's Armies.

"Go ahead, beg God to be merciful to you! But when you bring that kind of offering, why should he show you any favor at all?" asks the Lord of Heaven's Armies.

"How I wish one of you would shut the Temple doors so that these worthless sacrifices could not be offered! I am not pleased with you," says the Lord of Heaven's Armies, "and I will not accept your offerings."

— MALACHI 1:6-10

God not only said there's a blessing for giving, He said there's a cost when you give lousy offerings, *"Go ahead and ask me to be merciful to you and see. You're not in covenant with me. I want honor. And honor is expressed financially."*

"God so loved the world that He gave..." You can give without loving, as in Malachi 1, but you cannot show love without giving.

People who love NASCAR pay lots of money for NASCAR tickets and apparel. People who love the NFL will pay $350 for a ticket, $80 for parking, and walk two miles in the freezing cold to sit in 0°C (32°F) temperatures for four and a half hours with a smile on their faces. These people love their sport and are happy to pay the price. But many of those same people won't put $5 in a church offering.

When someone has a problem with giving, no matter how they clean it up, no matter how good they make it sound, their money is their god. They don't let it go, like Anna and Elsa from Disney, who gave good advice in that song. "Let it go. Let it go. Don't hold it back anymore."

Prosperity doesn't just mean money. You prosper in many other ways, but you can't leave money out. It includes money after your silver and gold have multiplied with everything else—that's in Deuteronomy 8.

Are offerings in the Bible, or were they invented by American preachers? They're in the Bible. The reward system for offerings is in the Bible. It was not invented in America.

QUESTION 27

ARE OFFERINGS PART OF A FINANCIAL REWARD SYSTEM?

I f you are critical of prosperity preachers, you probably hate when preachers say, "I feel the anointing." I'm sure you've never felt it, but I feel the presence of the Lord. I'm not just mindlessly saying what I say. I'm telling you that the Bible says that when you become a giver, *you'll have sufficiency in all things and may abound to every good work.*

> *Being enriched in every thing to all bountifulness, which causeth*
> *through us thanksgiving to God.*
>
> — 2 CORINTHIANS 9:11 (KJV)

> *But this I say, He which soweth sparingly shall reap also sparingly;*
> *and he which soweth bountifully shall reap also bountifully.*
> *Every man according as he purposeth in his heart, so let him give;*
> *not grudgingly, or of necessity: for God loveth a cheerful giver.*

And God is able to make all grace abound toward you; that ye,
always having all sufficiency in all things, may abound to every
good work.

— 2 CORINTHIANS 9:6-8 (KJV)

God doesn't want a casino built in eight months while the church raises money for 25 years and pays double what the church building is worth to a bank. Why should bankers sit in a glass skyscraper while the church is poor? Do you think that's the will of God? No, God's will is *that you may abound to every good work.*

(As it is written, He hath dispersed abroad; he hath given to the
poor: his righteousness remaineth for ever.
Now he that ministereth seed to the sower both minister bread for
your food, and multiply your seed sown, and increase the fruits
of your righteousness;)
Being enriched in every thing to all bountifulness, which causeth
through us thanksgiving to God.

— 2 CORINTHIANS 9:9-11 (KJV)

Knowing that whatsoever good thing any man doeth, the same shall
he receive of the Lord, whether he be bond or free.

— EPHESIANS 6:8 (KJV)

Seed time and harvest: What you make happen for others, God will make happen for you. And according to Christ, He'll do it in a multiplied fashion.

Mark 10, beginning in verse 28, will tell you the same thing; Jesus promised a hundredfold return. That wasn't made up on Christian television.

Enriched in everything.

Did Jesus talk about money? He sure did.

Are offerings in the Bible? They certainly are.

Does the Bible teach that offerings bring a financial reward to the giver? It certainly does.

God never spoke about you planting seeds in His kingdom without also talking about a harvest coming to you personally.

QUESTION 28

DOES THE BIBLE CHALLENGE PEOPLE TO GIVE BEYOND THEIR COMFORT LEVEL?

I s anyone in the Bible ever challenged to give beyond what they were giving? Can you imagine if they reported 1 Kings 17 on CNN?

> *Then the Lord said to Elijah, "Go and live in the village of Zarephath, near the city of Sidon. I have instructed a widow there to feed you."*
>
> *So he went to Zarephath. As he arrived at the gates of the village, he saw a widow gathering sticks, and he asked her, "Would you please bring me a little water in a cup?" As she was going to get it, he called to her, "Bring me a bite of bread, too."*
>
> *But she said, "I swear by the Lord your God that I don't have a single piece of bread in the house. And I have only a handful of flour left in the jar and a little cooking oil in the bottom of the jug. I was just gathering a few sticks to cook this last meal, and then my son and I will die."*
>
> *But Elijah said to her, "Don't be afraid! Go ahead and do just what you've said, but make a little bread for me first. Then use what's left to prepare a meal for yourself and your son. For this is what*

the Lord, the God of Israel, says: There will always be flour and olive oil left in your containers until the time when the Lord sends rain and the crops grow again!"
So she did as Elijah said, and she and Elijah and her family continued to eat for many days.

— 1 KING 17:8-15

Nowhere in the Bible is prayer used as a seed for financial breakthroughs or financial miracles. A person has to give financially.

Praise ye the Lord. Blessed is the man that feareth the Lord, that delighteth greatly in his commandments.
His seed shall be mighty upon earth: the generation of the upright shall be blessed.
Wealth and riches shall be in his house: and his righteousness endureth forever.

— PSALM 112:1-3 (KJV)

Who's it talking about? *Blessed is the man that fears the Lord and delights in his commandments.*

Note: Here, God sanctions wealth and riches for the righteous man. How foolish to condemn riches and classify rich men as wicked just because of their prosperity. Wealth is a blessing if used as God intended. It was God's original plan that all men be prosperous and use all things in creation for their own good and God's glory. That is still God's purpose. When the Messiah reigns, every man will sit under his own vine and victory, which shows there will be universal peace and prosperity.

It's not wrong to challenge people to give higher; it's wrong not to do so.

Are offerings taught in the Bible as a financial reward system? Were people ever challenged to give more than they were comfortable giving? Elijah certainly pressed the widow. And when she objected, he pressed even harder. When Paul did it to the entire church of Corinth, he basically shamed them for their paltry giving and told them to get with the program. It's not wrong to challenge people to give higher; it's wrong not to.

There used to be rabble-rousers pretending to be me on Instagram, telling people, "If you'll give $100, I'm going to pray a prayer of blessing over you." Some people do that—I don't. That's not a new problem, and it's not Biblical.

In the New Testament, specifically in the book of 1 Timothy, the Apostle Paul warns Timothy about false teachers who preach the gospel for personal gain. In 1 Timothy 6:5, Paul says, *"and constant friction between people of corrupt mind, who have been robbed of the truth and who think that godliness is a means to financial gain."*

Furthermore, in verse 10 of the same chapter, Paul says, *"For the love of money is a root of all kinds of evil. Some people, eager for money, have wandered from the faith and pierced themselves with many griefs."*

So, according to Paul, there are indeed people who preach the gospel intending to get rich, and he warns against them as false teachers who have strayed from the truth of the gospel. It was wrong then; it's wrong now. But it does nothing to undermine the Bible doctrine of prosperity or challenging people to step up to a higher level of giving.

QUESTION 29

WERE SIGNIFICANT GIVERS HONORED BY GOD IN SCRIPTURE?

Jesus stood by the treasury and watched what people put in the offering. After everyone gave, He singled out a woman for giving more than others; they chipped off some of their excesses, but she gave everything she had.

> And Jesus sat over against the treasury, and beheld how the people cast money into the treasury: and many that were rich cast in much.
> And there came a certain poor widow, and she threw in two mites, which make a farthing.
> And he called unto him his disciples, and saith unto them, Verily I say unto you, That this poor widow hath cast more in, than all they which have cast into the treasury:
> For all they did cast in of their abundance; but she of her want did cast in all that she had, even all her living.
>
> — MARK 12: 41-44 (KJV)

When Jesus had finished saying all this to the people, he returned to Capernaum. At that time the highly valued slave of a Roman officer was sick and near death. When the officer heard about Jesus, he sent some respected Jewish elders to ask him to come and heal his slave. So they earnestly begged Jesus to help the man. "If anyone deserves your help, he does," they said, "for he loves the Jewish people and even built a synagogue for us."

— LUKE 7:1-5

The man was honored because he was different. He stood out and was deemed deserving of recognition.

 Significant givers are noted throughout the Bible.

So why is it wrong for me to honor people when they give? If Jesus took note of significant givers and significant givers are noted throughout the Bible, why is it wrong for a ministry to send a thank-you gift to recognize significant givers?

QUESTION 30

DID GOD PROMISE TO MEET OUR BASIC NEEDS BUT CONDEMN ADDITIONAL FINANCIAL DESIRES?

Here, we see why the Devil goes against the teaching of prosperity because he doesn't want people to believe they can ask and believe and aspire to go higher.

> *Delight thyself also in the Lord: and he shall give thee the desires of thine heart.*
>
> — PSALM 37:4 (KJV)

> *If ye then, being evil, know how to give good gifts unto your children, how much more shall your Father which is in heaven give good things to them that ask him?*
>
> — MATTHEW 7:11 (KJV)

Did God promise to meet only our basic needs but condemn anyone who desired beyond that?

Tell God what you want Him to do for you.

God placed His nature within us, and God's nature is to reach higher. God was in Heaven and wasn't satisfied. So He wanted an Earth and man and a relationship. He's a creator, and He said, *"Be fruitful and multiply."*

QUESTION 31

IS IT IMPOSSIBLE TO INCREASE MATERIALLY AND NOT LOVE MONEY INSTEAD OF GOD?

I'm happy to warn any rich person in a meeting. The Bible says the desires of this life and the cares of this world will choke out the Word of God if you're not careful.

> *He also that received seed among the thorns is he that heareth the word; and the care of this world, and the deceitfulness of riches, choke the word, and he becometh unfruitful.*

> — MATTHEW 13:22 (KJV)

"If God blesses you, money will start taking the place of God." That's what I was taught in church growing up. If God blesses someone, then that money will take the place of God. It absolutely can happen. I think that's one thing that people don't understand about a preacher like me. They think I don't know any of the Scriptures that are in the Bible that are warnings to the rich.

"Lest when thou hast eaten and art full, and hast built goodly houses, and dwelt therein;
And when thy herds and thy flocks multiply, and thy silver and thy gold is multiplied, and all that thou hast is multiplied;
Then thine heart be lifted up, and thou forget the Lord thy God, which brought thee forth out of the land of Egypt, from the house of bondage;"

— DEUTERONOMY 8:12-14 (KJV)

The Bible says in Deuteronomy 8, *after I've multiplied your silver and gold, along with everything else, that's the time to be careful.*

But thou shalt remember the LORD thy God: for it is he that giveth thee power to get wealth, that he may establish his covenant which he sware unto thy fathers, as it is this day.

— DEUTERONOMY 8:18 (KJV)

Make sure you never say, "It was my own strength and ability that got me this wealth." Always remember it is the Lord your God who gives the power to create wealth.

So what did God say? He said you need to be careful. He didn't say it's automatic.

 You can love Him more when you're rich than when you were poor and never backslide.

What did Abraham prove? Abraham is proof that you can love God with all your heart, and as God makes you rich, you can love Him more when you're rich than you did when you were poor.

QUESTION 32

DOES GOD LOVE SAVING MONEY MORE THAN HE LOVES YOU?

God never revealed Himself in the Bible as Jehovah Bargoni, the God who gives good deals. It doesn't make any difference to God whether you fly in coach, business class, first-class, or have your own plane. It's your choice.

As a young preacher, I observed two people living in sin, getting drunk in first class. Walking to my seat in coach, I mumbled under my breath, "That's not right. I'm going to preach the gospel. I'm flying 11 hours in coach. These people are boozing it up, not married, kissing each other, and flying first class." The Lord spoke to me clearly, "I don't remember booking your airplane ticket. You did it yourself. You live how you want to live."

 God cares about what's best, not what's cheapest.

Do you believe God loves saving money more than He loves you? What do you think is more important to God: The money it costs to fly in business or first class, or my spinal health?

Do you think God saw His Son whipped on His back until they ripped it wide open so I could be healed, but then has a problem with me spending a few thousand dollars to fly 17 hours to India in a lay-flat seat? Or do you believe He'd prefer that I arrive in India looking like the third guy from the left on the evolution chart? If you think God wants to save money more than He loves you, then you don't know God.

> *"So if you sinful people know how to give good gifts to your children, how much more will your heavenly Father give good gifts to those who ask him."*

> — MATTHEW 7:11

QUESTION 33

DO YOU FIND IT STRANGE THAT YOU HOLD THE SAME BELIEFS AS THE HEATHEN ENEMIES OF THE CHURCH?

For all the articles they write in the New York Times questioning how a Christian justifies voting for Donald Trump, the answer is simple: witches are against him. They got together—all over the country—and cursed Donald Trump. The pornographers are against Donald Trump. People who promote wickedness of all kinds are against Donald Trump. The abortion industry is against Donald Trump. So, without even knowing anything about Donald Trump, if I know who doesn't like him, I know whether or not to like him. This is true for everyone, not just Donald Trump.

What sorrow for those who say
that evil is good and good is evil,
that dark is light and light is dark,
that bitter is sweet and sweet is bitter.

— ISAIAH 5:20

If I was for what wicked people were for, I'd check what side I was on.

For those who hate the prosperity message, do you find it strange that demonized people who hate the church share your sentiment about offerings and giving? I would. If I was for what wicked people were for, I'd check what side I was on.

QUESTION 34

ARE YOU CONCERNED THAT YOUR MINISTRY REQUIRES SUPPORT FROM PEOPLE WITH MORE THAN ENOUGH?

S ome preachers speak strongly against the prosperity message. "I don't believe in prosperity—it's an American gospel," they say.

I've thought about these things. That's why I chose my side—the right side. I didn't simply side with the denomination. I want to read the Bible, I want to have everything the Bible says, believe everything the Bible says, and preach everything the Bible says.

> *Their loyalty is divided between God and the world, and they are*
> *unstable in everything they do.*
>
> — JAMES 1:8

The President of the Bible college I went to once preached a harsh message against prosperity. He called it "this health and wealth gospel." After finishing his diatribe, he said, "Students, this school needs $3 million to repair a bunch of roofs and buildings. And if we don't get it, it could shut the school down." He said, "We need $3 million. We're going to pray right now that God gives us $3 million."

Well, which one is it, my friend? You just got done knocking prosperity. You don't believe in prosperity. Then you pray God gives you $3 million. A person who thinks like that has a mental problem.

 ## Where do you think money comes from?

He had an earned doctorate. I'm not sure what his doctorate was in, but I'm sure it wasn't in logical thought. Where do you think the three million's going to come from? Do you think a pornographer is going to give it? Is the mafia going to give it? Will a drug cartel give it, or do you think it'll probably come from a Christian who believes in Bible schools and preachers? If there were lots of people who had money to give and believed in the work of the Lord, would that make things easier for you or harder?

QUESTION 35

HOW MUCH DO YOU PERSONALLY GIVE?

I wish there were a prerequisite requiring anyone who posts a negative comment about prosperity to also include how much money they give each year. I expect the amount would rhyme with hero—as in zero. If it wasn't zero, it wouldn't be much more than that.

So-called Christians who hate the message of prosperity do so for the same reason wife-beaters don't want to hear preaching about not beating your wife—you're supposed to love your wife as Christ loved the church. People get convicted, and they don't like that. People like going to a church that doesn't speak against their personal sinful behavior. People who hold on to their money don't want to give and don't want to hear about giving.

How much do you give? That is the key question I have for those who hate the prosperity message.

 What God has done for others, he'll do for you.

God is raising up a new generation. I saw an interesting study claiming nearly 70 percent of Christians in the United States believe giving an offering causes the Lord to bless you financially. So for as much as people try to fight against the prosperity message, they are losing the battle because the young generation believes it—45 and younger. God is raising up Kingdom financiers.

What happened when Peter allowed Jesus to use his boat as a platform to preach the gospel? Jesus didn't just give him his boat back. Jesus gave him his boat back with a prophetic instruction. When Peter followed that instruction, after not catching any fish all night, he caught so many fish it nearly sunk his boat and tore his nets. That's a supernatural increase.

Everything God touches grows. Everything God touches becomes fruitful and multiplies. In a nutshell, that's why I believe in prosperity with all my heart. God spoke about it. God confers it on those who follow His commands.

Some churches say you can honor God with your time, your treasure, or your talents. That's what comes from weaklings too afraid to talk about money because money is all of those things in one. It takes time and talent to get the treasure. That's why sowing financial seed into the kingdom of God is precious and why God multiplies it back to those who give. Those who give never need to pray against personal poverty—poverty loses their address. When you give, as the Lord has instructed you to give, God said, *"The windows of heaven come open and pour you out a blessing that's so great you won't have enough room to take it all in. Try it and let me prove it to you,"* in Malachi 3:10.

If you're a typical Western Christian, you eat like an elephant and poop like a cat—consume, consume, consume; then you chip off a little for the Kingdom. Life gets hard when you live that way. But when you make large moves to advance the Kingdom of God, everything turns around. It doesn't just turn around for you, the blessing goes to your children, and your children's children. One man can change the situation of his entire family.

> *"If your faith is suppressed by negative teaching that to desire better things and a better life is wrong, then you'll waste your life and die in resignation and religious failure."*
>
> — T.L. OSBORN

Don't let religion neuter you. Dream big, do big. You can believe for God's best. You can have God's best. People should be able to enjoy God's best. But they'll never know God's best unless somebody preaches it to them.

By giving, the Lord increased us. And the same God that increased us will increase you. That's what Paul said.

> *And this same God who takes care of me will supply all your needs from his glorious riches, which have been given to us in Christ Jesus.*
>
> — PHILIPPIANS 4:19

AFTERWORD

For those who hate the prosperity message, I've just asked you 35 questions. For most of them, you have no answer because you've never thought about the question. For others, cliches and pat answers came to your mind because those are the things people told you. But I challenge you, let go of your past beliefs, attitudes, and behaviors, and reform your belief around the Word of God!

Praise the Lord!
How joyful are those who fear the Lord
and delight in obeying his commands.
Their children will be successful everywhere;
an entire generation of godly people will be blessed.
They themselves will be wealthy,
and their good deeds will last forever.
Light shines in the darkness for the godly.
They are generous, compassionate, and righteous.
Good comes to those who lend money generously
and conduct their business fairly.
Such people will not be overcome by evil.

Those who are righteous will be long remembered.
They do not fear bad news;
they confidently trust the Lord to care for them.
They are confident and fearless
and can face their foes triumphantly.
They share freely and give generously to those in need.
Their good deeds will be remembered forever.
They will have influence and honor.
The wicked will see this and be infuriated.
They will grind their teeth in anger;
they will slink away, their hopes thwarted.

— PSALM 112

Hatred and disdain for the message of prosperity is not an academic problem; it's a spiritual problem.

 "The wicked will see this and be infuriated. They will grind their teeth in anger..."

You may read this book, and if you're honest with yourself, you can't point to a time when you ever prayed the prayer of salvation. You don't need to *"slink away, their hopes thwarted."* Maybe you're tired of repeating empty cliches, or you've grown cold toward God. You can know you're saved and live a prosperous life. The Revival Today Staff is available to pray with you. Call the number below to talk to a real person who cares about you and who will pray with you and for you. It's the most important decision you will ever make!

Call 412-787-2578

"They themselves will be wealthy, and their good deeds will last forever."
Receive that into your spirit today.

AUTHOR PHOTO

"MY GENERATION SHALL BE SAVED!"

— JONATHAN SHUTTLESWORTH

ABOUT THE AUTHOR

Evangelist and Pastor, Jonathan Shuttlesworth, is the founder of Revival Today and Pastor of Revival Today Church, ministries dedicated to reaching lost and hurting people with The Gospel of Jesus Christ.

In fulfilling his calling, Jonathan Shuttlesworth has conducted meetings and open-air crusades throughout North America, India, the Caribbean, and Central and South Africa.

Revival Today Church was launched in 2022 as a soul-winning, Holy Spirit-honoring church that is unapologetic about believing the Bible to bless families and nations.

Each day thousands of lives are impacted globally through Revival Today Broadcasting and Revival Today Church, located in Pittsburgh, Pennsylvania.

While methods may change, Revival Today's heartbeat remains for the lost, providing biblical teaching on faith, healing, prosperity, freedom from sin, and living a victorious life.

If you need help or would like to partner with Revival Today to see this generation and nation transformed through The Gospel, follow these links...

CONTACT REVIVAL TODAY

www.RevivalToday.com
www.RevivalTodayChurch.com

Get access to our 24/7 network Revival Today Global Broadcast.
Download the Revival Today app in your Apple App Store or Google
Play Store. Watch live on Apple TV, Roku, Amazon Fire TV, and
Android TV.

Call: 412-787-2578

f facebook.com/revivaltoday
X x.com/jdshuttlesworth
instagram.com/jdshuttlesworth
youtube.com/@jonathanshuttlesworth

DO SOMETHING TODAY THAT WILL CHANGE YOUR LIFE FOREVER

THUS SAITH THE LORD, **MAKE THIS VALLEY FULL OF DITCHES**. FOR THUS SAITH THE LORD, YE SHALL NOT SEE WIND, NEITHER SHALL YE SEE RAIN; YET THAT VALLEY SHALL BE FILLED WITH WATER... **THIS IS BUT A LIGHT THING IN THE SIGHT OF THE LORD**... AND IT CAME TO PASS... **THE COUNTRY WAS FILLED WITH WATER**.

2 KINGS 3:16-18; 20

Revival is the only answer to the problems of this country - nothing more, nothing less, nothing else.

Thank you for standing with me as a partner with Revival Today. We must see this nation shaken by the power of God.

You cannot ask God to bless you first, prior to giving. God asks you to step out first in your giving - and then He makes it rain. We are believing God for 1,000 people to partner with us monthly at $84. Something everyone can do, but a significant seed that will connect you to the rainmaker.

IF YOU HAVE NOT YET PART-NERED WITH REVIVAL TODAY, JOIN US TODAY!

This year is not your year to dig small ditches. When I grew tired of small meetings and altar calls, I moved forward in faith and God responded. God is the rainmaker, but you must give Him something to fill. It's time for you to move forward! Will you stand with me today to see the nations of the world shaken by the power of God?

Revivaltoday.com/give

revivaltoday.com/paypal

Cash App $RTgive

venmo @RTgive

Text "RT" to 50155
Call at (412) 787-2578

Mail a check to:

Revival Today P.O. BOX 7
PROSPERITY PA 15329

REVIVAL TODAY Email: info@revivaltoday.com